TAORMINA

and surroundings

D1488177

Published and printed by

plurigraf

NARNI - TERNI

INDEX

Surroundings

Text: Loretta Santini
Revision: Anna Caprespa

© Copyright by CASA EDITRICE PLURIGRAF
S.S. Flaminia, km 90 - 05035 NARNI - TERNI - ITALIA
Tel. 0744 / 715946 - Fax 0744 / 722540 - (Italy country code: +39)
Printed: 2000 - PLURIGRAF S.p.A. - NARNI

PREFACE

The aim of this guide-book is to point out to the visitor the most interesting features of Taormina and nearby towns, such as Castelmola, Giardini and the ruins of Naxos, Letoianni, Forza d'Agrò, Capo S.Alessio and Randazzo. We shall also describe some other places renowned for their natural beauty and landscape, and finally say something about Mount Etna.

Taormina stands on the slopes of Monte Tauro, at about 200 metres above sea-level. It is the delightful "queen" of this promontory, jutting out into the Ionian; an enchanted place, with a quiet dreamlike atmosphere. With its many terraces facing out on to the sea, Taormina is both simple and aristocratic, intimate and charming. It witnesses to ancient prosperity and to eternal natural beauty. The remains of a glorious past have come down to us, and remind us of the finest moments of its history, but we can also appreciate it for its world renown as an elegant tourist resort. The town's animation is provided by the variegated colours of the flowers that abound in its quiet backstreets, but also by the many-coloured puppets ("pupi") which are to be found in its chaotic little bazaars. The sun always shines here - a statistical fact, since the percentage of clear days in the year is very high. Standing as it does near the heart of the Mediterranean, Taormina enjoys a very mild climate; it smiles out at the sea, lying on the last outcrop of the Peloritan Mountains which are covered with luxuriant vegetation, and sweep down to the Ionian near the mouth of the Alcantara (the river which separates them from the cone of Mount Etna). The first Greek settlers landed here. They found a natural environment that was more generous than elsewhere, and the place became one of the cradles of western civilisation. For this reason, we shall describe the Greek era in some detail when we talk about the history of Taormina. It was one of the most fortunate moments in the life of this town and its environs. The importance of this period is incomparable, and merits our close attention. However, there is another period which is worth mentioning, in terms of what still remains of it in the buildings and the town plan of

Taormina; this is the period when the Norman, Suabian and Aragonese dynasties ruled Sicily. The geographical position of Sicily, almost at the centre of the Mediterranean Sea, has always been a decisive factor in the history of this island. Since it was the meeting-point of various routes, it was influenced by a variety of civilisations and peoples. And the eastern coast of Sicily in particular, where Taormina lies, was more open to such influences than the other areas of the island. It seems certain that the isolated character of the island did not favour human settlement: until the neolithic age, the traces of human settlement along the coast are very rare. Then a population of farmers and shepherds, the Sicans, arrived and settled here, bringing with them influences from Mesopotamian civilisation, in the eastern regions of the island, closer to the mainland.

And it was here too that later on, around the 13th or 12th centuries B.C., the more developed Sicels introduced both the horse and the use of copper. They expanded rapidly, mainly thanks to the Aegean civilisation which was being spread at that time by the Phoenicians. Traces of the presence of the Sicels have been found near Taormina, specifically in Cocolonazzo di Mola, where there is a necropolis on a rocky hilltop. It is clear, however, that the particular historical association of these places is with Greek colonisation. The peoples from Greece who were expanding towards the west met up with the already flourishing coasts of Sicily. The first settlers were most probably from Chalcis in Euboea. They had already gone beyond the straits, and colonised Cuma and the Neapolitan archipelago, and they had come into contact with the Etruscans by the time they founded their first Sicilian settlement, Naxos, in 734 BC. Naxos was situated just south of Taormina, on the small peninsula of Schisò, near the beginning of the valley of the Akesinas, today called Alcantara. Its spirit lives on

through the remains which have been found near Giardini. It was founded by Theocles from Chalcis, but destroyed by Dionysius of Syracuse in 403 BC. The colony was in a fairly defensible zone, which enjoyed considerable prosperity thanks to the fertility of its lavic soil, and also to its geographical situation, not far from the Straits of Messina, which favoured trade, and penetration into the hinterland through the Peloritan mountains and Mount Etna. Before the Chalcidean people

they founded Catania on the slopes of Mount Etna in 728 BC, and a little further to the south they established Leontini.
The towns founded by Naxos undoubtedly flourished more than their parent city - exactly the opposite of what happened in the case of most of the other cities, notably Syracuse.
The political leader of the Greek colony of Taormina was Andromachus, who was able to set up an effective administration; he introduced a political constitution which made all public offices elective.

settled here, the area was under the influence of the Sicels, who did not, however, prevent them from settling. The Siculi of Tauromenion (on the site of present Taormina), came into close contact with the Greeks. Tauromenion itself finally became a colony, populated by the inhabitants of Naxos who had left their town when it was devastated by Dionysius. Naxos was mainly a religious centre, whose commercial and political development was very limited. The settlers from Naxos expanded in other directions:

He defended the town against the attacks of the Carthaginians and allowed hoplites sent to help the colony from the motherland to land there and settle. Initially these colonies lived mainly by agriculture, but in a development that lasted a century or more, they eventually became real commercial centres. They traded with the Italians, the Phoenicians, the Etruscans and of course with the inhabitants of their own motherland. The Sicilian towns exchanged the produce of the land, together with artefacts such as

Phoenician fabrics and Spanish glass. Trade often determined the position and expansion of Greek colonies. Their power grew so great that it exceeded that of their parent lands. The towns were politically independent, almost all of them dominated by a landowning aristocracy which limited the freedom of the settlers who landed in later periods, thus creating a conflict of interests. Slowly, however, the social situation changed along with the development of trade. The various colonies grew independent of each other, but this individualism was also a cause of their decline, when they failed to find the strength to unite against Carthage and Rome. The collective name for the Greek settlements in Sicily and Southern Italy is "Magna Graecia". The name is justified by the considerable material and spiritual development of these colonies; most probably it is here that the roots of our western civilisation are to be found. It is not easy to establish how independent Magna Graecia was as far as philosophy and art were concerned; how much it drew from the local populations and how much from Greece and the Greek colonies of Asia Minor. However, the colonies were quite distinct from the motherland. Orphism and Pythagoreanism, which had so much influence on ancient philosophy, both originated in these Greek colonies, though the philosophical currents which developed here were not exclusively mystical and metaphysical. It was a golden age for philosophy and art. Even today, the sublime poetry of the ancient flourishing civilisation is relived among the ruins of the Greek theatre of Taormina, and amid the walls of Naxos. Sicily became a Roman province after a long series of wars. It played the role of the "Granary of the Empire", and most of its territory was considered as "ager publicus" (common land). Tauromenion joined forces with Rome, since its support permitted the Greek town to check the expansionist policies of Syracuse. For this reason it was given the status of "free and confederate", a privilege bestowed on very few towns. Thus Taormina flourished economically. Some

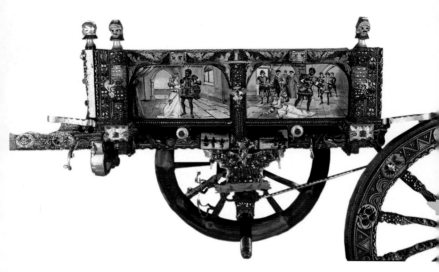

aqueducts were built (their remains can still be seen) and the Greek theatre was modified to the form we can still see today. Another striking fact is that the Romans began to consider it as a holiday resort and appreciate its beauties; they built fine villas in and near the town. The island was the scene of events which influenced the politics of Rome itself, among them the famous Servile Wars, when ancient Taormina was in a leading role. In 34 B.C. Octavian was defeated near Tauromenion during the war against Sextus Pompeius. Later on Octavian (Augustus) himself settled a colony here for strategic reasons. Apart from the events of political history, another very important factor was the decline of the remarkable ancient urban organisations, once sources of civilisation and culture. Under the Latin power these were reduced to relatively prosperous rural centres, whose importance was very limited, and hardly worthy of their

ancient splendour. From the 9th century AD, Taormina was considered to be the Byzantine capital of Sicily, thanks to its historical and strategic importance, but also to its magnificent buildings. In 902 it was captured by the Moslem invaders, but it continued to resist until 962, when it had to surrender definitively. After this came the Normans, and the inheritance of the Moslem rulers passed into the hands of Roger of Alteville. As always in the past, the history of Taormina was closely linked to that of the whole island. In 1079, after five years of siege, Roger conquered the city. Later, after the "Sicilian Vespers" of 1282, Taormina passed under the rule of the Aragonese. A very important event took place in 1410, when a Sicilian Parliament met in the Palazzo Corvaja in Taormina and elected Federico di Lana, the heir of Martin II, as independent King of Sicily. The whole period from the Norman conquest to the Aragonese era is of great importance because both Taormina and Randazzo are rich in remains from that age, especially the churches and palazzi. The architectural monuments of the Norman-Suabian style are especially worth noting, for they are emblematic of a kingdom which was known for its tolerance, and which assimilated elements of Greek, Latin, Arabic and Norman culture. The Byzantine influence, on the other hand, was felt most in the religious architecture, and particularly in the small churches which are often in the shape of a Greek cross with three apses. Moslem, local Gothic and Lombard Romanesque traces can also be found in some of these churches (especially Santa Maria in Randazzo). Various elements of Byzantine and Arabic culture flowed into the aesthetic forms of Norman art; otherwise all trace of them might have been lost in Sicily. During the 15th and 16th centuries, Taormina like the rest of the island was hardly influenced at all by the classicism of the Renaissance, and Catalan-Gothic remained very much alive. Even when the art of the Renaissance began to influence Sicily, it failed to produce really significant works. Baroque art, on the contrary, developed very strongly in the following two centuries, especially in the eastern and southern parts of the island, to such an extent that Acireale to the south of Taormina is full of baroque buildings. From the time that Taormina fell into the hands of foreign powers, it had almost no history. It was no more important than any other provincial town, and it no longer flourished until it underwent a revival in the last century. There was nothing but the memory of its prestige and fame. The town only began to flourish once more when the tourist industry developed; the name of Taormina came to be known all over the world as a holiday and tourist resort. Landscape and art drew many tourists here, and they contributed greatly to the local economy, in contrast with the sad condition of the inland areas that have long been centres of poverty, emigration and demographic decline. It was the Romans who first thought of Taormina as a holiday resort. When artists came to Italy in the 18th and early 19th centuries to discover the traces of the classical age, they naturally came here, but it was only at the end of the last century that the town became better linked to the mainland of Italy, and could be reached more easily by aristocratic and wealthy people, who were the first tourists in the area. The city became a small aristocratic resort, the summer residence of an exclusive population of kings, noblemen and important businessmen. Nowadays it has lost most of this air, because tourism is now open to all. However, the percentage of long-term visitors is small; most tourists only pass a day or two in Taormina.

THE GREEK THEATRE

The theatre is a masterpiece of Greek art; the art which reached forms as highly developed as the parallel advances in religion and philosophy. It was exported to the shores of southern Italy, and laid the foundation of a new patrimony of art and culture by means of superb, well-defined figurative forms. It is the result of the translation of highly sophisticated concepts into figurative language, as taught by immortal masters such as Phidias, Skopas, Praxiteles and Lysippus.

Even in the theatre itself, we find the canons of perfection, of immortalised pure beauty and mystical serenity far removed from everyday passion, which were so dear to Greek artists. They conveyed their artistic notions to Magna Graecia, where art was conceived as harmony and freedom, characterised by solemnity and purity - a vision which was to be of lasting importance to the whole of western humanity. Here in Taormina, one of the cradles of a new civilisation, we

find an expression of the flourishing Greek culture of that age in the theatre. Its value is enhanced by the skilled wedding of two factors - aesthetic sense and functionality - brought together in harmony for all to enjoy.

The theatre stands on a hillock dominating the town, where the spectator's eyes can sweep over the Greek remains and the fine natural landscape created by the seashore and the austere heights of Mount Etna.

The best viewpoint to appreciate the scenery is from the terraces to the side of the proscenium or from the top of the cavea (the horseshoe-shaped auditorium);

from here the landscape forms a backdrop to the ruins of the stage. The exceptional acoustics and the pleasing situation of the theatre, together with the atmosphere created by the ancient structures, are features which enhance the performances which take place here, still of a very high standard even today.

The original Greek construction dates from the third century B.C. In the second century of our era, the Romans modified the upper part of the cavea and the proscenium, the front of which was moved towards the orchestra and beautified by additional columns. The cavea was surrounded by an arcade which de-

fined its outer limits. Little remains of the original structures and of the spirit which inspired the Greek architects, unless we except the modulation of the cavea and the little channel which crosses the orchestra, probably used as in the theatre in Syracuse, for scenic effects and hydraulic purposes. The diameter of the theatre is 109 metres, while the orchestra is 35 metres wide. It could hold about 5400 people.

The cavea, which follows the hollow shape of the ground, is subdivided radially into nine wedge-shaped segments by small flights of steps. Five passages divide it horizontally into tiers. Some of the steps in the central sections have recently been restored.

In the wall which surrounds the cavea on the outside there were eight doors corresponding to the flights of steps which divide the cavea. Between the doors there were niches with statues. On the outside the cavea was surrounded by a double portico. The vaulting of the innermost portico supported a gallery for women, while the vaulting of

the outer portico supported a second order of galleries, higher than the others, and intended for the plebs or common people.

The stage consisted of a scenic wall enclosing a passage. In the wall there were three doors with niches containing statues between them.

In front of it, nine columns supported a portico. A second rank of columns in Corinthian style, like the others, completed the stage.

The columns which can now be seen were erected in a different position from the original one during a clumsy restoration in the nineteenth century.

At both ends of the scenic wall are two "rooms" (the parascenia") used as a storehouse for the equipment for the stage sets and the actors themselves. This is all that remains of the stage, and only the wall is in a good state of preservation. The "pulpitum" - the actual stage - was removed when the Romans turned the theatre into an amphitheatre.

Once it had been removed, the orchestra could then be transformed into an arena.

The orchestra which we see now is thus not the original one, but an enlarged one built during the Roman transformation. In addition, a "podium" (raised platform) was erected to protect the public, since the Roman entertainments were often quite risky for the spectators - we have only to think of the gladiator's fights and *naumachiae*, etc. Finally, we may note that a passage without a vault runs around the lower part of the steps of the cavea.

Access to the cavea and the terraces for women and plebs was by three flights of steps. Near the theatre there is a small museum (the Antiquarium), where various archaeological finds are displayed. They include interesting fragments of the ancient history of Taormina.

The Greek theatre of Taormina is a splendid specimen of Greek architecture, but it is not merely to be seen as an ancient monument and witness of the past. Its extraordinary functional qualities are constantly ready for exploitation, and it has excellent acoustics.

The spectator can hear the words spoken by the actors on the stage even from the highest ranks of the cavea, and catch the whole gamut of

tones. But while this is one of the main factors that have induced the City Tourist Office to bring the theatre back into use, there have also been other contributory factors.

The first of these is an aesthetic one: the wonderful harmony between the arches, columns and ruined walls of this architectural masterpiece and the backdrop provided by its remarkable position is a unique factor, a quite exceptional circumstance which gives a special quality to the musical and artistic performances and plays staged here.

Another factor - less visible but no less important - is the mysterious charm of these ancient ruins, which witness to a history and civilisation in which harmony was a rule, and art took on extraordinary new forms.

A new dramatic art form was created, and this theatre is its temple.

PALAZZO CORVAJA

In Piazza Vittorio Emanuele, in the area formerly occupied by the Roman Forum, stands the Palazzo Corvaja, once known as the Palazzo del Parlamento.

It was built in the 15th century on the site of an earlier (14th century) construction.

It takes its name from the Corvaja family, which only came to own it in the 16th century.

In 1410, Federico di Luna, the successor of Martin II of Aragon, was elected King during a meeting of the Sicilian parliament which took place in this building.

His "reign" was very short, but the palazzo has survived with its "Ghibelline" (swallowtail) battlements, with side lobes added. Half way up the façade runs a cornice with Latin moralising inscriptions.

On the main frontage, the cornice is surmounted by mullioned windows with two lights and pointed arches; on the top floor there are three rectangular windows with lower arches.

Below the cornice of pumice and lava stone, there are four rectangular windows.

On the side facing the church of Santa Caterina, there is only one elaborately worked window with three lights, and a doorway in the Gothic-Catalan style. Beneath its arch, tracery twists and rises to meet in the centre, supporting a coat of arms above the entrance door.

Passing through this doorway, we enter a picturesque and interesting courtyard.

There is a staircase built in the 14th century, leading to a gallery with window-sills decorated with bas-reliefs of biblical episodes.

A door with a pointed arch opens on to the small gallery.

To its right is a mullioned window with two lights, at the base of which is an inscription with the words *"Esto mihi locum refugii"* (Be a refuge to me), in the centre of which is a roundel of the sacrificial lamb.

Outward view of Palazzo Corvaja.

THE ODEON

In 1893 the ruins of the Odeon, or Little Theatre, were brought to light in the area behind the church of S.Caterina.

"Odeon" meant a small theatre used for musical performances. Its architectural form is more or less that of a common Greek theatre; however, this particular Odeon was built during the Roman imperial era by using already existing structures from an old temple, dating from the Hellenistic period.

It is a brick building, later enclosed by other construction work.

The cavea, with its classical semicircular shape, is formed of sixteen ranks, and these were divided into five sectors. A central passage led to the lower part of the cavea, while a second circular passage, surrounding the whole construction on the outside, led to the upper ranks of the cavea. The semicircular orchestra had a diameter of 11 metres.

The stage consisted of a wooden platform supported by a wall, remains of which are still visible.

The upper part of the stage consisted of the remaining portion of the Greek temple, particularly appropriate for this function because it was peripteral in shape (the term refers to temples in which a circular or rectangular cella is surrounded by columns).

The pre-existing Greek building was rectangular, and its longer side was used to build the stage of the Odeon.

The steps and the remains of some columns are almost all that survives of this part of the theatre.

The ruins of the "parascenia", the rooms for actors and stage equipment, are still standing.

THE NAUMACHIE

This is a magnificent Roman building, of which the upper part surrounding a large cistern still remains. The brickwork is 122 metres long and 5 metres high. Harmony is added by 18 large, apse-shaped niches, and some smaller rectangular niches, rather as if it were a nymphaeum (a classical construction of the Hellenistic-Roman period, with niches, columns and scenographic ple. They were quite widespread in the first century A.D., but by the 3rd century they had almost disappeared. The arenas were flooded for the purpose, with the use of a network of pipes. Real miniature ships were used, and slaves took part in the battles. It was one of the many diversions for public entertainment devised by the Romans.

This Naumachia, however, seems

water-displays). The façade of the building, however, is ruined by houses which have been built up against it. It was only in 1953 that restoration work began, to make the Naumachia more visible. Part of the pavement, with polygonal slabs, has been brought to light.

Although it is called "naumachia" (which means a naval battle), it does not seem that special shows of this kind took place here. In classical times, these "naumachiae" were held in amphitheatres for the amusement of the peo-

to have been used as a gymnasium. In ancient Greece the gymnasium was the place where athletes practised their sports, totally unclothed (gymnos = naked). It was also the place where young people and adults met for discussion, and where wise men and philosophers did their teaching. In terms of architecture, the exercise area and the baths of the Roman Gymnasia were particularly developed, thus differing from the Greek model, as described by Vitruvius and others.

THE CATHEDRAL (SAN NICOLÓ)

Built in the 12th century over an existing church, it was rebuilt during the 15th and 16th centuries and remodelled in the 18th.

Externally the severe lines recall those of Norman cathedrals elsewhere. The façade has a doorway dating from 1636, flanked by two ogival windows with single lights, above which is a small 16th century rose window with delicate tracery.

Inside, the nave and the two

aisles are divided by two rows of marble pillars supporting pointed arches.

The nave and transept have wooden ceilings of exposed beams supported by corbels with Arabic-style carvings.

The Sacristy houses a valuable collection of gold jewellery from a variety of periods.

Above: The triptych of the "Madonna with Child", four Saints and a Pietà, by Antonello de Saliba (1504).

Below: The Visitation with St. Joseph and St. Zachariah, a work dating possibly from 1457 by the painter Antonino Giuffrè.

THE PALACE OF THE DUKES OF ST. STEPHEN

Near Piazza del Duomo is the palace of the Dukes of St. Stephen. It was built at the turn of the fifteenth century, and belonged to the Spanish Dukes of that name. It has a quadrangular base, and its overall appearance is that of a tower.

The interior is divided into three areas, corresponding to three large rooms, one above the other. A doorway with an ogival arch leads to a hall on the ground floor, with cross-vaulting supported by a column in the centre of the room. On the outside, the hall of the room above is marked by a series of twin-light windows with pointed arches, two for each side of the palazzo. Exclusively on the façade where the main entrance is, we find a single light window at a lower level than the others. Further up, a narrow cornice runs at two thirds height, and on this rest the bases of a second rank of bigger and more ornate windows than the others.

A sharply pointed arch, with various types of tracery, surrounds each window, and also encloses a star-shaped window and both lights. Further up again, emphasising the upper limits of the building, is a broader two-coloured reticulated cornice supported by a series of small trilobe arches which give it lightness and relief. The reticulation is due to the mingling of lava and limestone.

At the side of the palace an external staircase led to the first floor, and on the same side, between the twin-light windows of the upper rank, a window with a rounded arch has been added.

BADIA VECCHIA

The Badia Vecchia, or Badiazza (the old abbey) is a rectangular building dating from the 14th century. It has three storeys. Looking at the main façade we can see an inlaid cornice of lava-stone and pumice on the upper storey. Above this are three ogival mullioned windows with triple lights, and small trilobe arches surmounted with little rose windows divided by groups of semi-columns in white marble. Above the Gothic window arches is a geometric design, also in lava and pumice, which adds grace to the upper part of the façade. Crowning all there are classic battlements of swallowtail design. On one side of the building an external staircase reaches to the first floor, opening into it through a door flanked by two double light windows of quite distinct design from each other: one has a rounded arch decorated with twin-toned cross ribbing, while the other has trefoil arches and an elegant little rose-window in marble (the window's overall shape is pointed Gothic). A recent restoration has brought back something of its former beauty. Its appearance of an austere but elegant tower gives the building a somewhat similar appearance to the palace of the Dukes of Santo Stefano. It is not known for certain by whom the Badia was occupied in the past; some claim that it did once function as a monastery, and hence the name.

Piazza IX Aprile - The elegant Café Chantant in the setting of the many-coloured pretty group of houses amid the greenery of the plants and the colourful flowers.

PIAZZA IX APRILE

The Piazza gives the impression of being a big panoramic terrace, from which a broad view over the town, the theatre, and the coastline can be enjoyed: in the distance, Etna also rises. At the end of the piazza there is the Clock Tower, or Porta di Mezzo. This is a mediaeval structure, but it underwent many changes in later epochs. It is crenellated, and in addition to the clock, it has a doorway with a rounded arch in its base section.

Piazza IX Aprile - evocative views.

THE HOTEL ST. DOMINIC

The deconsecrated convent of St. Dominic was transformed into a luxury hotel in 1895, and has a position with a wonderful view.

It seems a modest building on the outside, but the interior is a hotel of the highest class.

Right:
The interior of
St. Dominic Cloister.

THE CLOISTER OF ST. DOMINIC

The perfectly preserved cloister of the former convent of St. Dominic, with the sixteenth century arcading of its portico, the well, and the carefully tended vegetation of the garden, still offers to-day's visitor the enchanted atmosphere of monastic serenity. In addition to this cloister, which is the biggest, there are several smaller ones which are also highly evocative.

CASTELMOLA

Castelmola is reached by a road that winds up the rock for several kilometres, ending at the cliff where the town is perched at 500 metres a.s.l. Standing on its rock overlooking Taormina, it is a small but gracious village of little more than 1000 inhabitants, made up of picturesque houses divided by the narrow little streets.

These are worth a calm leisurely visit, because they offer delightful and captivating glimpses to the visitor. Above all, the place enjoys a wonderful open view over Taormina, the castle and the unforgettable spectacle of Etna in the distance. The Café San Giorgio, the panoramic terrace, and the ruins of a 16th century castle are the most characteristic and famous attributes of this place.

The castle itself deserves a separate mention, though unfortunately very little of it remains; even so it is a high point of the visit to Castelmola; hidden away in a green park it stands at the highest point of this rocky peak of the Peloritani. The dizzying view down the precipice from here takes the breath away.

It is like a natural fortress placed for the defence of Taormina against the forces of the hinterland. In the course of history it was fought over again and again, just because of its strategic position, so difficult to attack from below and so high that it could dominate the land as far as the horizon.

Some scholars believe that it was the ancient Mylai. It was destroyed and rebuilt time and again, according to the throw of the dice, first during the Hellenic period, then under the Arabs. A visit to Castelmola may be complemented by a trip to the nearby castle of Taormina, and to Cocolonazzo di Mola.

The mediaeval castle, reached by the road which climbs to Castelmola from Taormina, is also placed at a fine panoramic observation point, on the summit of Mount Tauro at about 400 metres a.s.l. It is polygonal and austere, standing on the top of a sheer outcrop of rock.

Further along the road to Castelmola is Cocolonazzo, a name given to a place where there is a high rock on which stands a very ancient necropolis, a reminder of the presence of the Siculi who populated this eastern zone of Sicily from the 13th to the 12th centuries BC.

The picturesque rock, on which the village of Castelmola lies, dominates Taormina from behind it.

THE LIDO OF MAZZARÒ

In the inlet between two rocky promontories lies an inviting beach, one of the many enchanting, romantic corners of the much-indented coast of Taormina: the lido of Mazzarò.

One of the most famous seaside resorts, with excellent tourist facilities, its attraction lies in the incomparable beauty of its setting.

A smiling bay where the cliffs are reflected in a placid sea, whose waves carve away at the limestone, it is gay with the colours of the thick vegetation that reaches right down to the shore, mild in the gentle slope of the hills to the beach, and welcoming in its hospitality.

Behind the stretch of sand there is a small group of hotels, pensioni, and the Grand Hotel Mazzarò, where tourists can find relaxing surroundings and enjoy a peaceful holiday.

The mild, typically Mediterranean climate makes it possible to visit this area at almost any time of the year.

The lido has bathing facilities for the ever-growing number of visitors.

The best way to enjoy the beauties of this enchanted stretch of the Ionic coast is to take a trip by boat, either northwards towards the Bay of the Sirens, or southwards, rounding Cape Sant'Andrea, beyond which lies another wonderful beach closed off at the south by Cape Taormina itself with its "faraglioni", at the centre of which Isola Bella rises gracefully.

The Lido of Mazzarò is connected with Taormina by a convenient cable railway, or by State Road 114, or for those who want to enjoy a walk with a view, by a narrow lane which rises through the greenery as far as Via Pirandello.

On these pages: various aspects of the Lido di Mazzarò.

THE BAY OF THE SIRENS

Nature has been especially generous in her gifts in this part of Sicily, endowing it with wonderful stretches of coastline among steep cliffs, promontories and tranquil gulfs which conjure up real emotional responses in the visitor who has come to these beaches because of the great fame Taormina already enjoys all over the world. The beaches of Mazzarò, Spisone, Cape Taormina, Cape Sant'Andrea, Isola Bella, the Faraglioni, the wonderful caves and the Bay of the Sirens are all encounters offered by the incomparable beauty of these places.

The Bay of the Sirens, a dream-like name for such an evocative place, is another unexpected strip of sand along the much in-

dented coastline. The cliffs create inviting little ravines, into which the salt water creeps. Here, where the blue of the water is less intense and dazzling because of the algae and the depth of the seabed, the light, broken up into kaleidoscopic fragments, reaches right down into the depths and is refracted in the various shades of colour. It is a paradise for underwater fishing, and a splendid setting for yachting; it satisfies the tourist's thirst for beauty while giving deep satisfaction to the longer-term visitor. It is a gentle place of dreams, a gracious and lovely promontory in a turquoise sea.

And as the ancient myths relate, the incautious visitor may be lured by the sweet song which the ghostly inhabitants of these rocks emit, trapping his attention till he has no way of escape. Thanks to all this, the bay has merited its name, the Bay of the Sirens.

THE BLUE GROTTO

A short trip by boat brings the visitor to some sea caves of exceptional beauty, which are hidden among the rocky walls of Capo Sant'Andrea. Damp and dark and cool, they reverberate with the noise of the waves breaking against the stony shore. They are illuminated by a flickering light, reflecting the constantly moving surface of the water. The visitor enters this unpredictable form of the natural world silently, with a sense of reverence. The caves with their dark flowing colours provide a harmonious soundbox for the voice of the sea. It is from the Grotta Azzurra that the regatta sets out on 9th July, to honour San Pancrazio in traditional fishermen's style.

GIARDINI - NAXOS

Along state road 114, half way along the gulf between Cape Taormina in the north and Cape Schisò in the south, there is a delightful village which stretches along the shore.

Its most important activities are fishing, wrought ironwork, ce-ramics and terracotta, but the tourist industry has also developed here, for Giardini has become a substantial seaside resort, a quiet place for a holiday, capable of offering good hotels, a long beach with very fine white sand to enjoy the magnificent Si-

cilian sun, and a little harbour for lovers of sea sports, and all the best facilities for holidaymakers.

For very different, though equally compelling, reasons, a visit should not be missed to the archaeological area of Naxos.

One historical mention: it was from these beaches that Giuseppe Garibaldi sailed with 4200 men across to the mainland of Calabria on 18th August 1860. Giardini has set up a monument to this event.

The coast-line of Giardini-Naxos.

THE RUINS OF NAXOS IN GIARDINI

Naxos was the oldest of the Greek colonies in Sicily. It was founded by the first colonists on the Ionian coast of the island, the Chalcideans under the leadership of Theocles, in 734 B.C. They settled on the peninsula of Schisò to the south of Tauromenion, and north of the mouth of the Alcantara, near present-day Giardini. The site of their settlement was particularly fortunate because it was so easily defended, and because its lava soil was so fertile (these were colonies of people from an agrarian background),

and also because of the nearness of the focal point of trade in this area, the Straits of Messina. It did not develop very strongly from the economic and political points of view, but it expanded by founding

daughter-settlements such as Catania and Leontini (Lentini) destined to become more important than Naxos itself. It did, however, become a centre of religious activity: in the city, the altar of Apollo Archegetis, the patron of all Greek settlers, was erected. Its history ended abruptly when Dionysius sacked it in 403 B.C.; its inhabitants fled to nearby Tauromenion. Archaeological research has brought to light part of the surrounding walls which once protected the city and marked out its perimeter. They included the whole area of the peninsula, bounded on the north by the roadstead of Schisò and to the south by the Santa Venera stream, running north-eastward along the coast and parallel to the Santa Venera to the south. In the interior, a fourth side must have completed the pattern of the perimeter at about 0.5 kilometres from the coast.

In the southern part of the Schisò peninsula, a stretch of about 600 metres of the ancient city walls can still be seen today. They are 2 metres wide and built in lavic stone, and on the outside they appear as a skilled polygonal construction with sloping projections. In the stretch which lies at right angles to the Santa Venera stream, there are two gates at the corners, and traces of the

Temenos of Aphrodite can also be seen. The foundations of a temple and two ancient furnaces have also come to light. Other tracts of the town walls can be found near-er to Cape Schisò. The valuable archaeological finds are enclosed in a beautiful green park, a splendid setting for the wonderful remains of Naxos.

The excavations of Naxos.

Typical glimpses of Giardini - Naxos.

LETOIANNI

This is a small town with a marvellous scenic backdrop. It lies at the centre of a tranquil, open bay, and there is an extensive beach.

Behind it lies the modern built-up area, crossed in the centre by a stream, the Letoianni, which dries up for many months of the year.

It has excellent tourist facilities, especially for sea-bathers. The town's economy is mainly agricultural, but tourism is becoming an important additional factor.

FORZA D'AGRÒ

Perched on a hill at 400 metres a.s.l., it looks out on a wonderful view of the Ionian Sea.
It is reached by a road which leaves the main state highway near Capo San Alessio, and follows a panoramic route for 4 km until it reaches the small

town. Its mediaeval character is almost untouched; especially interesting the Gothic/Catalan gateway of Piazza SS. Trinità and the bell-tower of the 18th century parish church, while the castle has now been transformed into a cemetery, from where there is a splendid view.

CAPO SANT'ALESSIO

Continuing along state highway 114, which runs along the Ionian coast, nearer the sea than the motorway E45, Capo Sant'Alessio is met with not far from Forza d'Agrò. This lonely and austere point is incomparably beautiful; it stands out as a high, sheer rock rising from the sea, and there are the remains of a fine castle on its rocky heights. The ancient Greek colonisers called the rock *Argyrion Akron* - the Silver Cape. The castle, which cannot be reached from the sea because of the sheerness of the cliff, stands on the twin slopes of the promontory. On one of them is the section almost completely rebuilt by the English at

the beginning of the 19th century, in a circular plan of two cylindrical buildings superimposed on each other, surrounded by walls with narrow spyholes. On the other slope, there are the remains of the more ancient polygonal building, standing sheer above the sea. Walls join the two buildings into a single whole. The castle of Sant'Alessio has a feeling of bewitchment as it stands silent among the rough and straggly scrub clinging to the rock, where the crows have their nests, while the air echoes to the crashing of the waves below. A reef lies at the foot of this rugged promontory. Secret memories call to the visitor; far from the madding crowd, lost and solitary on a stretch of the coast which has retained its wild charac-

ter, this is one of the finest places on the whole coast of Ionia. Its character as a spur of isolated and unspoilt land has a mysterious fascination, as powerful as that of solitude itself.

Both an impregnable fortress and a magnificent viewing point, it is a sharp spur protruding into the Ionian, austere and enchanting at the same time, a place suited as a setting for a fairytale, for fantastic spells or meditation in the open air. Here nature gives a wonderful revelation of itself to those who look down towards the depths of the precipice from the castle above, giving the dizzying sensation which only a seagull in full flight can know, and compelling them to meditate on its amazing quality.

ETNA

Mount Etna is Europe's largest volcano. Since it is a volcano, its height has undergone many changes - for instance in 1900 it was 3274 metres (app.10000 feet) high, but in 1966 it was calculated at 3326 (an additional 150 feet). It takes the form of a large cone with more or less regular sloping sides; 900 or more secondary cones punctuate its surface, and the huge crater with high rocky walls several kilometres wide is known as the Valle del Bove, the valley of the Ox.

The true cone, however, begins at a height of 1500 metres, and is interrupted at 2900 metres where there is a high plateau corresponding to an ancient elliptical crater. From this plain the final cone rises. The base of Etna has a more or less circular perimeter of about 200 kilometres. The entire Etna zone is comprised between the Alcantara in the north and the Simeto in the south. The name

Etna may be derived from the Greek word meaning "fiery" or "flaming": it is also known as Mongibello, derived from the Arab word *jebel* which means a mountain. According to classical mythology, in the infernal bowels of Mount Etna was Hephaistos' (Vulcan's) forge, where he produced thunderbolts for the gods by hammering deafeningly on his immense anvil. Thus the shower of hot stones and fire which belched from the crater were for the ancients an expression of the work of the god, and of his sooty helpers the Cyclops. One-eyed giants, the Cyclops were those who made it possible for Zeus (Jupiter) to subdue the Titans, who tried to seize Mount Olympus. Envious of the power which the son of Saturn had conquered, they besieged the palace of the gods. Jupiter appealed for help to the Cyclops, who forged the thunderbolts from red-hot strips

of copper, and this was the weapon by which Jupiter gained the victory over the rebels.

The Titans survived their defeat (Typhaeus, Hephaites, Polybates, Encelades and Hyperbius) and were chained inside Mount Etna; from there, in their roaring rage they made the land around tremble. Pindarus, when he saw the volcano rising in isolation to its dizzy heights, thought - in one of his classic flights of fancy - that it should be called "the Column of the Skies; Goethe visited it, studied it and admired it, and Homer

and Hesiod speak of it. Pindarus and Aechylus described the eruption of 475 B.C.

In ancient times Etna must have had a luxuriant cloak of vegetation, but little remains of it, because of both human activity and volcanic eruptions. The highest area is completely denuded, deprived of all forms of vegetation, and only astragalus, tansy and three types of phenerogamic flora remain to bear witness of the former rich flora above the 2000 metre line. In the lower area, on the other hand, there is a fertile and productive zone, where extensive cultivation has gone on, especially of citrus and vines (the wines of Etna are of excellent quality). The lava, when it solidifies and is then broken up, creates quite fertile soil, but it is also a source of riches for the economy of the area because it is used for building materials, road surfaces and the chemical industry. The lavic stone is also found in many of the monuments of Taormina and nearby villages. While the annual rainfall on the slopes averages about 600-700 millimetres, it rises to as much as 1400 mm in the upper section, and this plentiful rainwater, enriched by that from the melting snows, is absorbed by the highly absorbent volcanic soil. It then re-emerges below 800 metres in the form of valuable reservoir supplies for agriculture. Etna is an active volcano; over 100 eruptions are recorded in history, but very probably there are others that have never been described, so that the number may be much higher. The most memorable in scope and violence were those of 1669, 1928 and more recently the very long one of 1951 and those of the 1980s. The stages of eruption, the secondary volcanic phenomena, the seismic and bradyseismic movements are the subject of great interest and research to experts. But Etna also attracts less serious interest, beckoning to the tourist to approach; it is the enveloping fascination of this mountain which both destroys and bestows life, and attracts when it is tranquil only to repel and drive away when it bursts into flame. It is a living mountain, which has stirred human imagination since the most ancient times. A solitary, majestic cone, standing out above the other peaks of the island, its summit is more than 3000 mt. above sea level and it is a look-out post over the whole of Sicily. Countless tourists climb up every day to see the crater, "the monster's mouth", amid the gases exhaled from its unplumbed depths.

Here are some practical suggestions for those who want to climb up to the summit. The lower station of the cable railway that reaches an altitude of 2504 metres is to be found at the Rifugio Sapienza. It takes visitors on a comfortable journey up to Piccolo Rifugio, the intermediary station, and from here it continues to its high point at 2935 metres. The cable railway thus reaches the base of the final cone, from where the ascent to the crater is only on foot. Once there, the eyes of the visitor are greeted with an incredible spectacle; if the sky is clear it is possible even to see Malta far to the south, Palermo to the west and to the north the Straits of Messina and the Aeolian Islands. A limitless horizon stretches out before our incredulous gaze.

The panorama almost makes one forget that we have reached the crater, smoking, exuding foul-smelling gases, constantly changing shape because of the activity of the volcano. There are many enthusiasts who attempt the final climb, right up to the highest peak, sure of finding refuge from the unpredictable caprices of the mountain in the shelters scattered around all over the place. Many excursions are possible along these denuded crags, in search of the evocative surroundings in which the volcanic activity reveals itself.

Right: Suggestive features
of Etna's activity.

RANDAZZO

A small town poised at 765 metres (2400 feet), with about 12500 inhabitants, it is rich in history and monuments. While it has remained unharmed for centuries by the volcano despite

its close proximity to the central crater, it was seriously damaged in the second world war by bombardments, and many of its monuments were irreparably disfigured. Despite this Randazzo still retains the charm of a mediaeval town, much of which is still unchanged. It is a fine example of the architectural and artistic achievements of the period from the 13th to the 15th centuries. The dominant feature is the severe array of mansions of noble families with their pointed arches and doorways, twin-toned friezes in lava and limestone. The ogival arch is also the dominant feature in the fifteenth and sixteenth century houses: in fact the influence of the Renaissance was felt very late on in Sicily, and lacked the expressive power to replace the Gothic style. However, there are some palazzi belonging to the Renaissance period, such as the Palazzo Clarentano (1509), though it is still more of a transitional example of the passage from mediaeval to Renaissance building styles. Many of the architectural and decorative features present in the buildings of Randazzo are similar to those found in Taormina. In this small town, everything points to its former splendour, from the time that Frederick III raised it to the rank of a duchy (1333) and it became the summer seat of the Aragonese court. Even today the streets still have that sharp flavour of the mediaeval; one need only walk around the via degli Uffizi or the via dell' Agonia to sense it, or pass in front of the oldest buildings: Palazzo Lanza, casa Spitalieri, Casa Cavallaro, Palazzo Spada and so on. Another interesting feature is the Porta Aragonese (1282), one of the entrances which gave access

through the walls of the town. It still bears the arms of Peter of Aragon. Randazzo's greatest moments are linked to the names of the Suabian and Aragonese dynasties.

The town was traditionally divided into three quarters - the Lombard, Greek and Latin - whose inhabitants spoke three different dialects, and attended three separate places of worship, the three churches of Santa Maria, San Nicola, and San Martino.

The Church of Santa Maria

The church of Santa Maria is in the Norman-Suabian style and was built in the fourteenth century, but little remains of the original structure, only the right hand side of the main body of the building and the three apses. Its appearance changed as a result of restorations in the 16th and 19th centuries.

The façade of the church was built around the middle of the 19th century. At the centre stands the bell-tower with its square base and polygonal spire. Three big pointed arches break up the lower section: above are two orders of single-light windows in pairs, and above that again a series of trefoils with rosettes. At the sides of the church are two large entrances with ogival arches. The grey metallic colour of the lavic stone contrasts with the white limestone with which the arches, doorways, spires and rosettes are trimmed, resulting in a harmonious overall appearance.

The right side is dominated in the centre by an austere entrance in the Gothic-Catalan style, dating from the 16th century. It has an architrave and is surmounted by two small windows, one above the other. In the upper one is a niche with a small Madonna in white marble,

the work of craftsmen from Pisa. The whole doorway is decorated with simple and twisted columns in clusters, capitals, and floral friezes. The doorway is reached by means of two opposite flights of steps.

The rest of the surface is uniformly regular, only broken in the upper section by a row of regularly set windows.

The three apses at the far end of the church are "disguised" as towers, crenellated at the top. Their upper surfaces are decorated with a checkerboard frieze in two colours. The left-hand side of the church dates from the 16th century and also has a large doorway in the Gothic style.

The interior is divided into three naves, separated by two rows of monolithic pillars in the classic metallic grey colour of lava stone, each with a decorated capital. The transept and dome are not part of the original plan of the building, but were added much later according to the favourite notions of the architects of the 19th century.

On the walls of the side aisles, corresponding to the chapels and the altars, there are numerous fine paintings. In overall terms the interior of the church seems to belong more to the sixteenth century than to the middle ages, but the nineteenth century restoration in fact altered the characteristic spirit of the building.

Left: The Church of Santa Maria - Interior.

Below: The Church of Santa Maria, view of the external side.

In the photographs: details of the doorways in the façade of the Church of Santa Maria. The capitals, rich with fine carving, show ornamental designs of flora and fauna; the overall impression is of a delicate drama in marble. The corbel representing an angel is also worthy of note.

The Church of San Nicola

Half-destroyed by the bombardment and then restored, all that is left today of the fourteenth century building is the apse and the transept, while the rest of the church dates from the 16th century. The belltower, of which the upper part is missing, dates from 1789, and the façade is 17th century. This is the largest of the three churches of Randazzo; we find many elements in it common to other buildings in the town: the use of twin tones and lavic stone, the apse with the battlemented tower. In front of the church stands a statue of Randazzo.

The Church of San Martino

Practically nothing remains of the original church, except the interesting bell-tower which still keeps its 14th century appearance. The façade dates from the 17th century; it is ponderous, static and sober. The frieze that crosses the façade horizontally should be noticed; it contains white marble panels dating from the Renaissance. Beside the church stands the belltower: it has two ranks of single light windows in pairs, with transversal dichromatic strips in lavic stone and limestone; above this is a rank of trefoil windows. At the crenellated tip of the belltower is a polygonal spire. The interior of the church has a nave and two aisles in 16th century style.

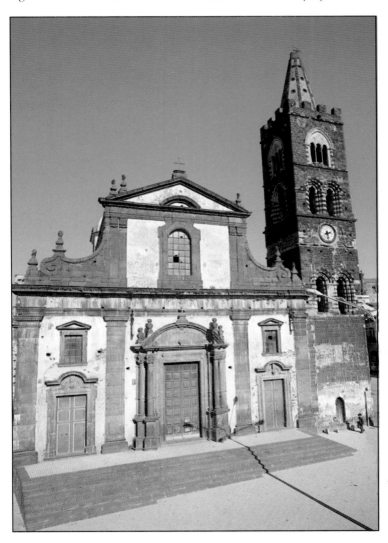

THE ALCANTARA VALLEY

The Alcantara is one of the most important all-the-year round rivers of Sicily.

From the original Akesinas, the name was transformed into Alcantara, meaning bridge in Arabic. 48 kilometres long, it rises in the mountains of Nebrodi, and in its short route to the sea, it passes through the valley squeezed between the Peloritani in the north and Etna in the south.

It is the third natural asset of the area, in addition to Taormina and Etna, because of its natural beauties such as the gorges of Larderia and the artistic treasures scattered in the valley, mostly belonging to the mediaeval period.

The economy of the whole valley is based on agriculture and cattle-rearing; only 10 percent of the soil provides any form of substance for its inhabitants, infertile as it is, and made up of volcanic folds. There are no industries, except for the fact that the Alcantara has made it possible to introduce hydro-electric schemes of great importance for the needs of the area. The river also provides another source of life: it makes irrigation for land use possible. Sources of irrigation are vitally important, and are nevertheless very scarce. This is a basically very poor region, where even commerce has not developed much; emigration has led to a constant bleeding away of its people, and the only resource, agriculture, is based on great and middle-sized estate ownership with many landless people employed to till the soil. From the touristic viewpoint, the Alcantara valley has much interest because of its historical and artistic monuments, grouped especially around Randazzo (described

elsewhere), and for the unusual feature of the Gorges, which are well worth a visit. The so called Gorge of the Alcantara is near the district of Larderia, a few kilometres away from the hydro-electric installations. A high narrow gorge (more than 60 feet tall and only a few feet wide) winds its way through the midst of abundant green vegetation.

Its main feature consists of the basalt prisms from which the walls of the gorge are formed; juxtaposed one on another, they form lines, sometimes straight and sometimes curved, and occasionally fan-shaped, giving character to the surface of the walls in a delicate sort of design. It seems as if a mediaeval cathedral is enclosing the narrow bed of the Alcantara between its gothic walls. Smooth natural apses are to be found everywhere, produced by millennia of erosion caused by the constant action of the water.

The river takes on glazed and changeable colours between the harsh, austere grey of the rocks. In places the water flows quietly and serenely, in others it breaks up into streamlets and small foaming waterfalls, whose caprices change the tone of the reflections of the light in a landscape which sometimes seems unreal. The gorge is carved into the lava slopes of Etna, shaped by the lava flows from the Molo crater. There are marvellous views both at the riverbed level and from the heights of the rocky basalt walls. In the periods in which the Alcantara is at low level and its depth is only a few centimetres, one can easily walk along the bed of the river and enter the hidden corners of the gorge by gazing up from below at the menacing rocks that rise almost vertically, hemming in the steep, tortuous passage. The strange shapes of the basalt rocks stimulate the imagination: the prisms which have settled along lines of force, crystalised at the moment when the boiling lava cooled, bring to mind the vibrant surfaces of a futuristic sculpture, while they seem to be in movement according to constant undulations, they are in reality fixed and immobile, in their majestic monumentality, like splinters jammed together and hurled from some unimaginable distance, so that they seem still to vibrate with the energy they once possessed. It is a place of wonders, and a source of amazement. It deserves appreciation, because it is frequently overlooked by hasty tourists who are attracted by Taormina and Etna, and forget this enchanted corner where nature has carved its own works of art on a grand scale. But even where the river flows through an open valley, the Alcantara offers attractive prospects as it rushes towards its outlet to the sea between its volcanic banks.

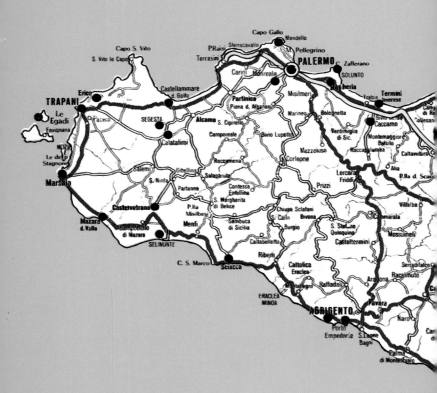

I. Ustica

Capo Gallo — Mondello
P.Raisi — Sferracavallo
Terrasini — PALERMO
Capo S. Vito — M. Pellegrino
S. Vito lo Capo — Carini — Monreale — Zafferano
Erice — SOLUNTO — Bagheria
TRAPANI — Castellammare d. Golfo — Misilmeri — Termini Imerese
Le Egadi — Paceco — SEGESTA — Partinica — Trabia
Favignana — Piana d. Albanesi — Caccamo
MOZIA — Alcamo — S. Cipirello — Marineo — Bolognetta
Le due Stagnone — Calatafimi — Camporeale — Bivio Lupotto — Ventimiglia di Sic. — Montemaggiore Belsito
Marsala — Salemi — Roccamena — Mezzoiuso — Roccapalumba — Caltavuturo
S. Ninfa — Gibellina — Salaparuta — Corleone — Alia — P.lla d. Scavo
Castelvetrano — Partanna — Contessa Entellina — Prizzi — Lercara Friddi
Mazara d. Vallo — P.lla Misilbesi — S. Margherita di Belice — Chiusa Sclafani — Villalba
Campobello di Mazara — Menfi — Sambuca di Sicilia — Carini — Bivona — S. Stef. Quisquina — Cammarata
SELINUNTE — Callabellotta — Burgio — Castelltermini — Mussomeli
C. S. Marco — Sciacca — Ribera — Serradifalco
ERACLEA MINOA — Cattolica Eraclea — Raffadali — Aragona — Racalmuto
Montallegro — AGRIGENTO — Favara — Naro
Porto Empedocle — S. Leone Bagni
Palma di Montechiaro

Pantelleria — I. Pantelleria
Montagna Grande